Also by Evelyn McFarlane & James Saywell

If . . . (Questions for the Game of Life)

If ^{2} . . . (500 New Questions for the Game of Life)

If ^{3} . . . (Questions for the Game of Love)

If . . . Questions for the Soul

How Far Will You Go?

How Far Will You Go?

Questions to Test Your Limits

Evelyn McFarlane & James Saywell

Photographs by Diana Stezalski

VILLARD / NEW YORK

Published in the United States by Villard Books, a division of Random House, Inc.,
New York, and simultaneously in Canada by Random House of Canada Limited, Toronto.

VILLARD BOOKS and colophon are registered trademarks of Random House, Inc.

Library of Congress Cataloging-in-Publication Data

McFarlane, Evelyn.
How far will you go?: questions to test your limits / Evelyn McFarlane and James Saywell.
p.   cm.
ISBN 0-375-50242-4 (alk. paper)
1. Conduct of life Miscellanea.   I. Saywell, James.   II. Title.
BJ1581.2.M243   1999
081—dc21   99-20344

Random House website address: www.atrandom.com
Printed in the United States of America on acid-free paper

2 4 6 8 9 7 5 3

DESIGNED BY BARBARA MARKS

Introduction

How large is your life? We are given so many opportunities to hear that question answered by others, famous people, people who do extraordinary things or to whom interesting and unique things happen. Yet rarely do we ask it of ourselves, or even of the people we know well and love. But our so-called everyday lives are still full of remarkable experiences, challenges, and amazing or even courageous accomplishments, large and small. We wanted to write a book of questions to find out about them, to discover the edges of our lives, to ask about the outer and inner limits that we have already experienced, or have yet to find.

If one's life can be measured in a sense by the distance between its extremes, then these questions are designed to reveal the surprising breadth of everyone's life, and to appreciate and celebrate the truly grand adventure of life itself. Never predictable, and always capable of astonishing us, our lives present us with the biggest adventures of all. Put yours to the test!

How Far Will You Go?

W hat is the one thing you'd *most* like to change about the world?

What do you want *most* right now?

What are you *most* grateful for?

What was the *warmest* welcome you ever received?

What was the *best* thing about your youth?
What was the *worst*?

When and where have you felt *most* uncomfortable
being nude?

Who is the *most* interesting person you've ever met?

What's the *most* imaginative thing
you've ever done as an adult?

4

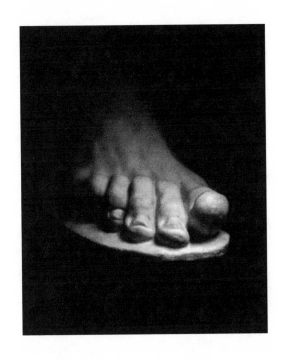

What is the *least* you've ever worn in public?

What is the *best* example of "perfection"
that you can think of?

In what way are you *least* understood?

Who is the person you miss *most* right now?

What was the *worst* vacation you ever took?

What is the one non-monetary thing you have the
highest hope of obtaining in life?

Where is the *dirtiest* place you've ever been?

When do you love yourself *most*?

6

What would you *most* readily die for?

What would you *most* like more sympathy for?

What is your *favorite* store in the world?

What was your *most* disappointing sexual experience?

What is the *strongest* opinion you hold?

What is the *most* difficult problem
you've ever had to solve?

When were you the *strongest* that you've
ever had to be?

What room of your home do you spend *most* time in?

Where would you *most* like to be right now?

What was the *biggest* sin ever committed against you?

What sin do you *most* enjoy committing?

What is the one thing you'd *most* like to be forgiven for?

When have you come *closest* to meeting the devil?

What is the *truest* example of compassion
you have ever witnessed?

Who is the person you know with the *purest* soul?

Who is the person *most* loyal to you?

What is the *greatest* thing you would sacrifice
to find true love?

Who made the *strongest* first impression on you?

What turned out to be the *most* useful course
you ever took in school?

Who has the *strongest* personality among
the people you know?

What is the *biggest* injustice you have ever suffered?

What single word *best* describes you?

What single word do you hate *most*?

On whom did you make the *strongest* first impression?

12

What is the *most* surprising action you've ever taken?

When was your life *most* out of control?

When have you been *most* honorable?

Who is the person *most* similar to yourself in the world?

Who is the person *most* able to make you laugh?

What is the *most* valuable thing you own?

In what way are you *most* humble?

What is the *best* way for you to relieve tension?

Which person have you taken *most* advantage of?

What is the *greatest* life-forming experience you ever had?

What subject would you *most* like to learn more about?

What would you be *best* at, were you to change careers?

Whose words or actions can you *most* easily predict?

Who in life have you felt the *strongest* need to protect?

What would you *most* like to be remembered
for after you die?

Whose smile can *most* easily persuade
or seduce you?

16

What is the *strictest* a parent should be?

What is the *hardest* thing about love?

What is the *cruelest* thing a person has ever said to you?

What is the recurring dream that you *most* enjoy?

With whom is your willpower *weakest*?

What are the *best* and *worst* letters you have ever
received in the mail?

What is the *best* thing you have ever won as a prize?

What is the *sexiest* thing anyone has ever worn for you?

What is the *strongest* willpower you've ever displayed?

What's the *worst* crime you have ever committed?

What is your *strongest* argument against capital punishment?

What have you done to *most* qualify you
as a white-collar criminal?

What would be the *best* way to get rid of a dead body?

What crime from history fascinates you *most*?

What is the *worst* punishment you've ever had to endure?

Who do you think was the *worst* criminal in history?

What true crime have you been *most* tempted to commit?

What was the *weakest* you've ever been?

What is the *strongest* profanity you use?

Who had the *best* body you ever made love with?

Who has the *weakest* set of values in your family?
And among your friends?

When do you have the *strongest* ability to concentrate?

When do you *most* need attention from your lover?

Who is the *dumbest* person you ever dated
more than once?

What is the *most* spontaneous you have ever been?

What was your *most* Freudian moment?

What is the *poorest* you've ever been?

What have you been *most* ignorant about in your life?

What in the world would you *most* like to see protected?

How do you waste the *biggest* chunk of time
each day or week?

What have you been *most* naive about?

What is the *most* interesting kind of life to lead?

Where would you *most* hate to be pierced?

Whose brain power have you found *most* intimidating?

What one word would you say *best* describes your country?

Who is the person *most* sensitive to your needs?

What's the *most* difficult confession you've
ever had to make?

What is the *most* painful thing a lover has ever done to you?

Who *most* deserves your love?

What is the *hardest* thing to forgive?

Who is the person you'd *most* like
to take revenge on?

What part of your day-to-day life requires
the *most* patience?

What is the *closest* you've ever come to being rich?

Who is the *scariest* person you've ever known?

Who was the *least* attractive person
you were ever attracted to?

What has been your *most* difficult breakup?

When were you the *least* virtuous?

What was the job you enjoyed *least*?

When were you *most* and *least* selfish?

What is the one thing about your country
that makes you *angriest*? And *proudest*?

What is the *best* thing you've ever done for your country?

What do you think is the *worst* thing about liberals?
And about conservatives?

What do you *most* want the current president to accomplish?

Who would you pick as the president
who did the *most* for the betterment of the country?

What issues are you *most* hypocritical about
when considering your own political views?

Which of your own qualities do you *most* want in a president?

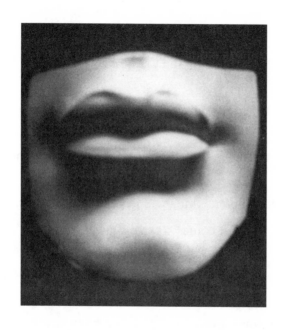

When do you find yourself *most*
politically incorrect?

When did you have the *weakest* self-confidence ever?

What is the *most* inexplicable thing you've ever witnessed?

What is the *least* gratitude you've ever been shown?

What is the one thing you have ever made or created
that comes *closest* to perfection?

In what way do you come *nearest* to your idea of perfection?

What thing about your family are you *least* proud of?

What topic do you feel *least* comfortable
discussing with your lovers?

What kind of power do you want *most*?

What's the *best* single piece of advice you ever received?

What's the *best* advice you didn't heed?

For whose life have you had the *most* sympathy or pity?

What has been the *biggest* accomplishment of your life?

What kind of cowardice do you *most* despise?

What was the *biggest* fight you've ever had with someone?

What's the thing you know the *most* about?

34

What is the *most* cowardly thing
you've ever done?

35

Who have you been *most* frustrated by in your life?

When were you *closest* to being a champion?

When were you *most* moved by a ceremony?

Who is the person you know with the *freest* spirit?

What is the *best* thing you've ever put in your mouth
first thing in the morning?

What was the *most* difficult choice
you were ever forced to make?

What is the *most* disturbing sound you know of?

What was the *best* gift you ever gave to someone?

What experience has made you *wisest*?

What is the *cruelest* thing you've ever suffered?

What's the *best* thing you've ever tasted?

In what way have you displayed the *best* taste?

What is the *worst* example of betrayal
that you have suffered?

What was the *hardest* decision you ever had to make?

What is the thing of *highest* value
that you have ever lost?

What is the single *nastiest* thing
you've ever done to someone?

What problem do you think is *most* common
among friends your age?

What is the *most* valuable quality in a friend?

What is the *strongest* quality in your best friend?

What is the *most* painful thing you've ever had to tell a friend?

What is the *biggest* favor a friend has done for you?

What is the *cruelest* thing you have ever done to a friend?

What is the one thing a friend has that you would
most like to have for yourself?

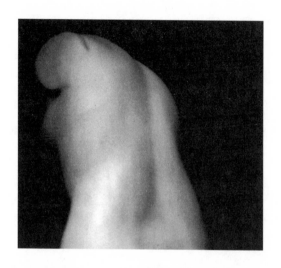

What is the *worst* character trait in a friend that you can overlook?

What are the cirumstances in which you
most resist change in your life?

What was the *best* toy you have ever owned?

When in your life have you felt *loneliest*?

What one thing would you *most* like to abolish?

What is your *strongest* emotion?

What is the *most* physical touching—other than with
your lover—that you feel comfortable with?

When did you need the *most* perseverance in your life?

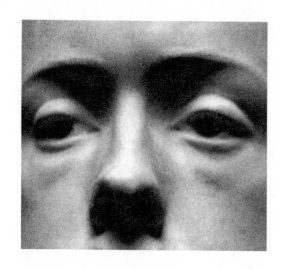

What is the *strongest* craving you get?

When were you *most* disappointed in yourself?

What is the *least* you expect from your kids
after they've grown up?

What's the *shortest* amount of time between orgasms
you've ever experienced?

Which law would you *most* like to change?

Who is the one person you have hated
the *most* in your lifetime?

What is the single *worst* thing about living
at this time in history?

What has disappointed you *most*?

44

What's the *best* way to commit suicide?

What is the *best* possible attitude toward death?

Whose job would you find *most* rewarding?

Who is the *least* generous of the friends you keep?

What's been the *longest* day of your life?

What has been the *best* year of your life so far?

What's the *shortest* time you've ever spent between meeting someone and having sex?

What is the *biggest* coincidence of your life?

What's the *oldest* you'd like to live?

Who is the *most* amazing woman you know personally?

What is the *best* position for sex?

What is the *least*-deserved praise you've ever received?

What's the *most* destructive argument you've ever had?

What was your *best* experience in school?

What is the *nicest* imperfection in your mate?

What's the *most* meaningful compliment
you've ever received?

When have you been *most* supportive of another person?

What is the *most* disturbing poverty you have ever seen?

What's the *best* thing to inherit other than money?

What is the *strongest* argument for why you deserve
the money you make?

What is the *least* amount of money you would
have to have to consider yourself rich?

What is the *easiest* money you have ever earned?

What is the *worst* thing you have done on account of money?

What is the *most* you've spent on something really stupid?

What is the *poorest* you could be and still be happy?

In what way did you *most* worry your parents
while growing up?

What would you find *hardest* about being in prison?

What is the *most* satisfying thing you do each day or week?

Who is the person with whom you've been
most infatuated?

What is the one thing you are *proudest* of in life?

What is the *worst* prejudice you have ever endured?

What one thing would you *most* like to happen tomorrow?

What is the *most* indulgent thing you do each day or week?

What was the *worst* sexual experience you ever had?

What one thing would you *most* like to steal?

What is the *biggest* thing you have ever stolen?

In which part of your day does time go *slowest* and *fastest*?

What is the *most* sinful you've ever been?

Which sibling is or was favored *most* by your parents?

What is the *worst* emotional pain you've ever suffered?

W hose thoughts would you *most* like to read?

W ho is the person you'd *least* like to touch?

W ho is the person you know who you'd *most* like
to see naked?

W hat is the *worst* quality you inherited from your parents?

W hat has truly been the *most* embarrassing moment
in your life?

W ho is the person you'd *most* like to torture?

W ho is the friend you *most* often disagree with?

W hat is your *greatest* virtue?

What is your *best* vice?

What have you lost that you would *most* like to retrieve?

What is the *best* ritual of your daily life?

What is the *most* important action you've ever taken?

Who is the person you'd like to help *most*?

What is the *worst* thing you have ever said to your mother?

What is the *most* rebellious thing you've ever done?

What is the *most* rebellious thing you've ever wanted to do?

What is the *biggest* risk you've ever taken?

What is the *worst* thing about your present job? And the *best*?

What is the *most* useful job you've ever had?

What aspect of your job are you *weakest* in?

What's the *best* and *worst* thing about your boss?

What one person *most* affected the choices
you made in your career?

What is the *strongest* contribution you make
at your place of work?

What is the *least* amount of money you would take
to do your current job?

What is the *largest* decrease in wages you'd accept
to have a job you enjoy more?

What's the *biggest* surprise you've ever had in bed?

What is the *worst* physical harm you have ever
inflicted on someone?

What was the *truest* prediction you ever made or heard?

What is the *most* beautiful sound you've ever heard?

What is the *most* erotic scent you've ever smelled?

What is your *greatest* love story?

What was the *most* disgusting thing
you've ever had to do?

What is the *closest* you've ever come to death?

In which year of your life did you change the *most*?

What's the *worst* thing you could possibly hear
about your own child's personality?

Who is the person you *most* wanted to have
an affair with but didn't?

What is the quality in your father you would
most like to share?

Who is the person you'd *most* like to touch but never have?

What have you *most* envied in a sibling?

What's the *best* thing you've ever gotten for free?

64

When do you have the *most* difficult time telling the truth?

Who had the *most* enviable parents among your friends?

What do you *least* respect about your father?

What is the thing you're *best* at?

What dream are you *least* likely to ever forget?

What is the *most* original thing your mate has ever done?

When was the time that you could *least* believe your eyes?

Who of all your friends has the *most* power?

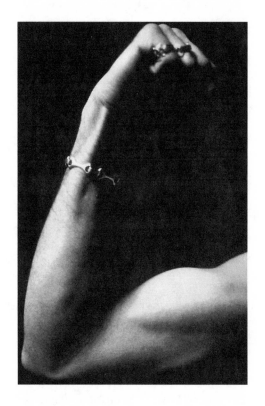

W hat's the *wildest* thing you've ever done in public?

W ho is the one person you have learned *most* from in life?

W hat is the *worst* thing you have to do each morning?

W hat invention of this century has had
the *biggest* impact on your life?

W hat is the single *most* important thing you have ever learned?

W hat was the *luckiest* moment of your life?

W hat do you have the *worst* reputation for? And the *best*?

W hat aspect of your reputation is *least* deserved?

What's the *most* daring sexual thing you've ever done with
someone of the gender you don't prefer sexually?

W hat is the *longest* amount of time you could spend
on a desert island with your lover or spouse
before needing the company of others?

W ho is the person you *most* regret having had sex with?

W hat was the *most* erotic moment in your life so far?

W hat is the *youngest* age at which people
should begin having sex?

W hat is the *youngest* age at which you could accept
your child having sex?

W hat's the *longest* you have ever been celibate?

W hat was the single *most* bizarre place you've ever had sex?

What is the *least* amount of money you would accept to never have sex again?

Of the people you know,
who has a natural sense of style you *most* envy?

What one thing in your life has caused the *most* harm
to your health over time? And the one that has been
the *most* beneficial?

When did you show the *most* courage ever?

Who is the person you can *most* easily anger?

Who was the *best* lover you ever had?

Who is the person you are *most* candid with?

What is the *most* amount of money you would spend for proof
if you suspected that your spouse was cheating on you?

72

W̶ho is the person you find *hardest* to please?

What one thing do you miss *most* about another place?

Who taught you the *most* about good sex?

What was the *hardest* secret you've ever had to keep?

What are you *most* underappreciated for?

What is the *most* sacred thing in your life?

What is the *biggest* lie you've ever been told?

What is the *grandest* lie that you've ever told?

What was the *hardest* apology you ever delivered?

What is the *biggest* bribe you have ever taken? And given?

What is the one thing you'd *most* like to forget?

What is the single thing in your life
you are *least* likely ever to forget?

What's the *most* cash you've ever held
in your hands at one time?

What is the *most* comforting thing you have in your home?

What one thing would you *most* like to teach
the opposite gender?

What is the *biggest* myth about sex?

76

What do you feel *most* guilty for in your life?

When, or on what subject, have you been *most* hypocritical?

Who is the *easiest* person to be with that you know?

What is your *biggest* self-doubt?

What was the *largest* debt you ever ran up?

Who was the *worst* creep you ever dated?

What is the *biggest* regret of your life so far?

Who is the *worst* enemy you ever made?

78

What is the *largest* sacrifice you ever made?

What is the one thing in life you care *most* about?

What is the thing that gives you the *most* joy in the world?

In what way are you *most* judgmental?

What do you *most* look forward to—and dread—
about growing old?

What was the *biggest* thing you ever got away with?

Where was the *farthest* from home that you've ever felt?
And actually been?

When were you *happiest* to come home?

What is the *worst* trouble

you've ever gotten yourself into?

When have you been the *most* shocked?

Who is your *greatest* hero from history?

What's the *best* telephone call
you've ever received or made?

What's the *greatest* event you ever attended?

What is your *shallowest* side?

What's the *best* thing you ever found?

Who was the *noisiest* partner you ever made love with?

82

When have you *most* shocked yourself?

Where in the world have you felt *safest*?
And *most* in danger?

When did you have the *most* fun in your life?

Who, among your friends, made the *worst*
first impression on you?

When have you been *most* silent?

Who is the person you make feel guilty *most* often?

What do you honor *most* in your mother?

What's the single *most* beautiful sight you've ever seen?

84

What was the *most* jealous moment of your life?

What's the *first* thing you notice in a person's appearance?

Which nationality do you find *best* looking overall?

What one part of your own body comes *closest* to your ideal?

What is the *dumbest* thing you do to make yourself better looking?

When did you look *most* beautiful (or handsome)?

When have you found it *hardest* to look at yourself in the mirror?

What physical characteristic could you *least* tolerate in a mate?

86

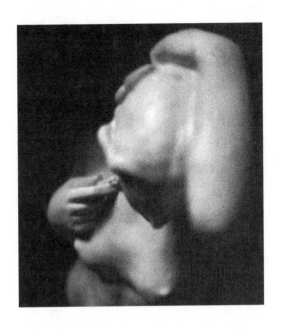

 What is the *most* extreme thing you would do to your own
appearance to make yourself better looking?

What's the *best* hiding place you know?

What is the *best* gift you ever received?

Whose absence have you felt *most* in your life?

What was the *best* wish you ever had come true?

What is your *favorite* form of play?

What is the single *most* beautiful word in your language?

What was the moment in your life
when you felt *most* in love?

88

In what way are you *most* self-disciplined?

What is the *worst* way you abuse your body?

In what period of history would you have *least* liked to live?

What life goal have you achieved *most* quickly?

What is the *best* manifestation of freedom in your life?

Who have you *most* feared in your life?

What do you feel is the *clearest* definition of virtue?

What's the *most* physically demanding sexual position
you've ever tried?

90

In what way are you *most* competitive?

What would make you go insane the *fastest*?

What was the *quickest* escape you ever needed to make?

What experience do you have the *greatest* fear of?

What is your *biggest* pet peeve?

What is the single *greatest* act of kindness
you have ever received from a stranger?

What do you hate *most* about ambitious people?
And like *most*?

At what time in your life were you *most* ambitious?

What one experience do you *most* desire
that you haven't yet had?

Whose talent, among the people you know,
do you *most* envy?

What is the thing you are *most* interested in right now?

What was the *quickest* friendship you ever made?

What was your *quickest* quickie?

What is the *best* thing to do right after sex?

What is your *strongest* reason for legalized abortion?
And against?

In what situations do you have the *least* control
of your emotions?

94

What's the *biggest* compromise you ever made?

What is the *best* quality you inherited from a parent?

What is the single *biggest* mistake you've made as a parent?

What was the *most* enjoyable year in rearing your child?

What is your *best* memory from childhood?

What do you think is the *most* difficult thing about being a teenager today?

What single word would you use to *most* accurately describe your parents?

What would you *most* like to hear from your father?

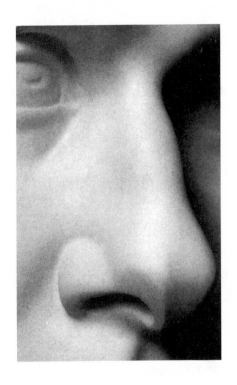

What is the *most* extreme thing you would do to alter your child's appearance before he or she reached puberty?

To whom do you talk *most* about sex?

What is the one thing that *most* pleases you?

What news do you *most* fear hearing?

What is your *worst* addiction?

What's the *biggest* advantage you have going for you?

What's the *boldest* thing you've ever done?

What do you *most* want to change in your life?

What do you *most* need to change in your life?

What is the *best* thing about your life?

What is the *best* thing about living at this moment in history?

What place are you *most* tranquil in?

What was the *worst* departure of your life?

What was the *best* arrival of your life?

What was the *worst* accident you ever experienced?

When has your intuition served you *best*?

In what situations do you exaggerate the *most*?

What habit would you *most* like to give up?

What's the *most* overused word in your vocabulary?

What deflates your self-esteem *fastest*?

In what situations do you *most* rely on your parents?

In what area of your life are you *neediest*?

Whose luck do you *most* envy?

What question do you avoid *most*?

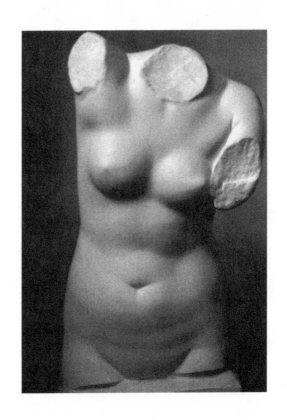

How are you *most* critical of yourself?

How do you flirt *best*?

What would you *most* like to change about men?
And about women?

What is the one thing you'd *most* want a therapist
to help you with?

Who is the *first* person you'd send to a therapist?

What is the *most* inexplicable thing you've ever done?

In what way are you *most* unique?

What is the *best* thing about being a man? And a woman?

What would you *most* like to stop?

What is the *biggest* mistake you've ever made in a relationship?

What is the quality you love *most* in your partner?

What is the *biggest* advantage you have over your lover?

What is the single *best* thing you've ever done for your mate?

What is the *most* difficult thing about being married?

What is the *strongest* part of your marriage?

What do you boast about *most* when you
want to impress your mate?

What would you *least* be able to forgive in your spouse?

What was the *biggest* bridge you ever burned?

Who was the *closest* thing to a sex addict
you've ever known?

What makes you *most* nervous?

What is your *biggest* contribution to the world?

What are you *most* greedy for?

What makes you lose your temper *most* easily?

What one natural thing would you *most* like to see?

What's the *furthest* you've ever pushed yourself physically?

What part of the female body fascinates you *most*?
And the male body?

What time of day do you *most* appreciate or need silence?

What is the *silliest* thing you own?

What is your *most* treasured possession?

What is the *wildest* thing you've ever done in a car?

What is the *worst* word anyone ever used to describe you?

What would you *most* like to change in your house?

Who is the person who *most* deserves to be rewarded for something?

What makes you *most* content?

What's the *best* game that you play?

What is the *most* useful article of clothing you've ever owned?

What is the *best* revenge you've ever taken on someone?

What is the *worst* revenge you've ever had to suffer?

What was the *best* example of the existence
of Fate or Providence in your life?

What is the *most* irrational action you've ever taken?

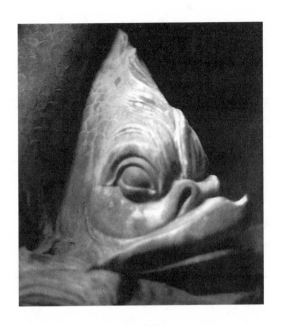

What is the *strongest* drug you have ever tried?

What is the *worst* habit you've ever had?

What was the *worst* experience you ever had
involving alcohol?

What's the *deepest* depression you've ever been in?

What was the *lowest* thing you've ever done?

What made your parents *happiest* about you as you grew up?

What is your *finest* quality, now, as a child to your parents?

What is your *best* quality as a parent to your children?

What is the *biggest* favor you've ever done for a friend?

What are the things you like *most* and *least*
about organized religion?

What would be the *worst* thing to be reincarnated as,
aside from a human being? And the *best*?

What is the *least* appropriate thing to pray for?
And the *most*?

What do you pray for *most* often?

Whose spirituality do you *most* suspect?

What tests your faith in a higher power the *most*?

Who is the *closest* thing to an angel you've ever known?

116

What is the *most* spiritual experience you've ever had?

What was the *most* romantic evening you ever had?

What was the *worst* weather you ever experienced?

What was the *worst* year of your life?

When were you *most* disappointed by a friend?

What is the *largest* amount of money
you ever made in one day?

What is the *most* annoying habit your mate has?
And how do you *most* annoy him or her?

What was the *greatest* number of times you had sex
in a single day?

118

What is the *highest* price you would pay for great sex?

What's the *weakest* excuse you ever used?

What is the *greatest* sacrifice anyone has ever made for you?

What has been the single *most* important influence
on your life?

What has changed or redirected your life *most* dramatically?

What is the *most* worthy cause on earth?

What is the *hardest* test you've ever taken?

What is the *most* important duty you perform
on a regular basis?

What was the *hardest* you ever fought for something?

In what situation would you *most* enjoy
being temporarily invisible?

What would be the *quickest* way to hell for you?

How could you *best* alter your karma?

Who is the *most* amazing relative in your family?

What is the *best* place to touch, and to be touched?

When did it take you the *longest* time to reach orgasm?

What was the *slowest* realization you ever came to?

What was the *most* difficult promise you've ever had to keep?

What is the *greatest* age difference you can imagine
tolerating in your own love life?

What is the *emptiest* part of your life?

What is the *least* amount of time you could spend with your
children each week before you would feel neglectful?

Toward whom are you *most* prejudiced?

What do you feel is the *most* noble profession in the world?

What is the *biggest* reward you would pay
to get your pet back?

What's the *hardest* question you've ever answered?

124

What would you *most* easily be driven to kill for?

What's the *biggest* surprise you've ever had?

What's the *biggest* failure of your life so far?

What is the *highest* praise you have ever received?

What is the *highest* praise you've ever given?

What is the thing you'd *most* like to begin?

What is the thing you'd *most* like to complete?

Who had the *best* responses to these questions?

126

W‍hat is the *fullest* aspect of your own life?

About the Authors

EVELYN MCFARLANE was born in Brooklyn and grew up in San Diego. She received a degree in architecture from Cornell University and has worked in New York and Boston as an architect. She now lives in Florence, Italy. In addition to writing, she lectures on architecture for the Elderhostel programs and paints.

JAMES SAYWELL was born in Canada and lived in Asia as a child. Besides questions, he designs buildings and furniture. He divides his time between the United States, Italy, and Hong Kong.